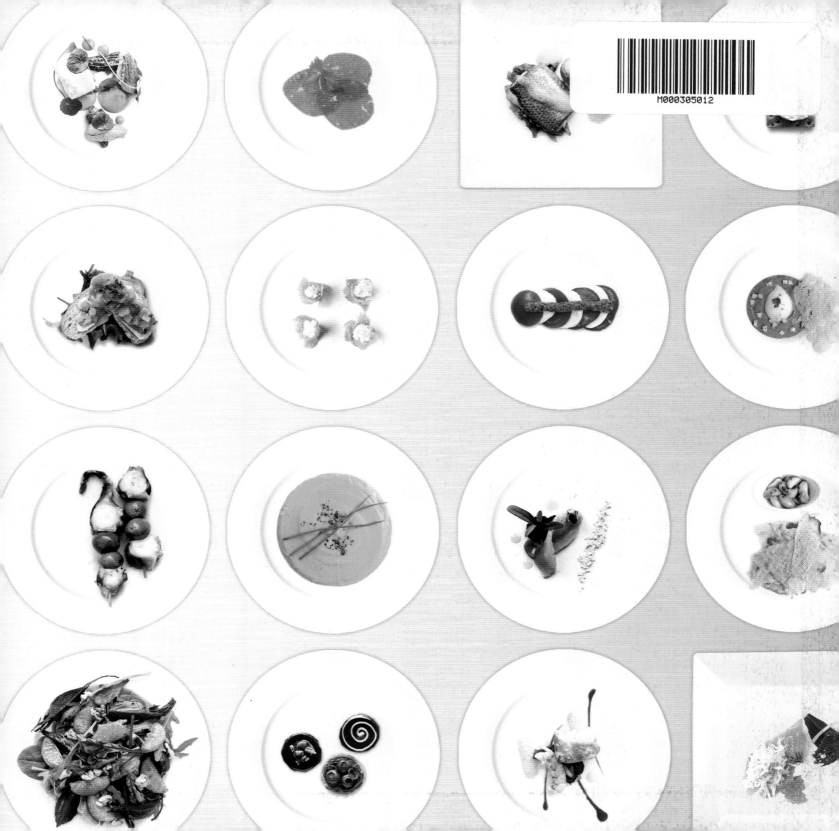

FOOD & ART
STYLING IDEAS

First published in the United States of America by Rockport Publishers, a member of Quayside Publishing Group
100 Cummings Center
Suite 406-L
Beverly, Massachusetts 01915-6101
Telephone: (978) 282-9590
Fax: (978) 283-2742
www.rockpub.com

ISBN: 978-1-59253-859-1

Digital edition published in 2014
eISBN: 978-1-61058-940-6

10 9 8 7 6 5 4 3 2 1

Design: Grip Design
Art direction: Kelly Kaminski, Kevin McConkey
Cover and interior design: Jenn McHale, Camay Ho

Printed in China

FOOD & ART STYLING IDEAS

MOUTHWATERING FOOD PRESENTATIONS FROM CHEFS,
PHOTOGRAPHERS & BLOGGERS FROM AROUND THE GLOBE

WRITTEN & CURATED BY
ARI BENDERSKY

DESIGNED BY
GRIP × CHICAGO

Rockport Publishers
100 Cummings Center, Suite 406L
Beverly, MA 01915

rockpub.com • rockpaperink.com

THE
MENU

WE ALL NEED FOOD TO SURVIVE, **but we should all, at some point in our lives, have the opportunity to experience truly gorgeous food that not only nourishes us physically, but also inspires us visually, emotionally, and creatively.** Whether plates are prepared through molecular gastronomy in the foremost restaurants around the globe or through simple, rustic methods in your own kitchen, beauty can lie within any preparation. As a society connected through social media, more and more people take and share photos of their food, further connecting us all through the love of the perfect bite. As a food writer and culinary explorer, I have had the privilege of feasting on wonderful dishes by some of the world's most renowned and respected chefs. Having the honor to gather the gorgeous images found on the following pages further fueled my desire to share the beauty that can be discovered through food.

For this collection, **we reached out to photographers, stylists, and gourmands around the globe,** both professional and amateur. People couldn't have been more thrilled to share their visual experiences with us and eventually with you to help inspire your next photo shoot, whether for yourself or a commercial endeavor. Photos came in from all over the United States as well as far-flung places like Kuwait, Estonia, Australia, Costa Rica, England and beyond, showing how similar ingredients can produce wildly different, yet equally delicious, results.

The following chapters showcase food in haute preparations as well as in its natural, organic state. From indulgent platings featuring juicy burgers piled high with melted cheese or sweet cakes *oozing* with chocolate sauce to healthy preparations of salads, vegetables, or grilled fish, *1,000 Food Art & Styling*

Ideas can help stimulate your creative juices and show you just how much fun taking photos of food truly can be. Spend time browsing the pages as you jump from Land to Sea, explore the use of Color, turn things up with Heat, or tell a story through Narrative. No matter how you thought of food before, you are surely bound to experience it in a new light and a truly altogether different flavor profile.

Get ready to have a heightened, sensorial experience and no matter how you let these photos inspire you, be sure you enjoy each and every savory shot. **ONE WARNING: Don't flip through these pages on an empty stomach as you may go on a dining binge.** And if you do, don't say we didn't warn you . . . the following pages contain serious drool-worthy images. **Enjoy!**

ARI BENDERSKY

COLOR

BRIGHT / BOLD / PLAYFUL

DAVE BRADLEY
USA

0001

HEATHER SPERLING
USA
0002

HEATHER VAN GAALE
USA
0003

JUSTIN B. PARIS
USA
0004

KATE RIESENBERG
USA
0005

SCOTT ERB AND DONNA DUFAULT
USA

0006

ERIC KLEINBERG
USA

0007

MOLLY MCMAHON
USA

0008

NADINE SHAW
AUSTRALIA

0009

ERIC KLEINBERG
USA

0010

GALDONES PHOTOGRAPHY
USA

0011

ELISABETTA REDAELLI
ITALY
0012

ERIC KLEINBERG
USA
0013

EZEQUIEL BECERRA
COSTA RICA
0014

CARA AND SCOTT NAVA
USA
0015

GRIP
USA

MOLLY MCMAHON
USA

0017

TY LETTAU
USA

0018

TY LETTAU
USA

0019

TY LETTAU
USA

0020

ERIC KLEINBERG
USA

0021

TUAN H. BUI
USA
0022

NADINE SHAW
AUSTRALIA
0023

HEATHER SPERLING
USA
0024

GLENN SCOTT
USA
0025

PARAGON MARKETING
COMMUNICATIONS KUWAIT
0026

TUAN H. BUI
USA
0027

TUAN H. BUI
USA
0028

MOLLY MCMAHON
USA
0029

AZITA HOUSHIAR
USA
0030

PARAGON MARKETING
COMMUNICATIONS KUWAIT **0031**

ELISABETTA REDAELLI **0032**
ITALY

TUAN H. BUI **0033**
USA

RUTH HUIMERIND **0034**
ESTONIA

TUAN H. BUI **0035**
USA

RUTH HUIMERIND **0036**
ESTONIA

HEATHER SPERLING **0037**
USA

TUAN H. BUI **0038**
USA

TUAN H. BUI **0039**
USA

NICOLE ZARATE
USA
0040

SHERI SILVER
USA
0041

HEATHER VAN GAALE
USA
0042

PARAGON MARKETING COMMUNICATIONS
KUWAIT
0043

ELISABETTA REDAELLI
ITALY

0044

TY LETTAU
USA

0045

ELISABETTA REDAELLI
ITALY

0046

HEATHER VAN GAALE
USA

0047

PARAGON MARKETING COMMUNICATIONS
KUWAIT
0048

MOLLY MCMAHON
USA
0049

HEATHER SPERLING
USA
0050

MOLLY MCMAHON
USA
0051

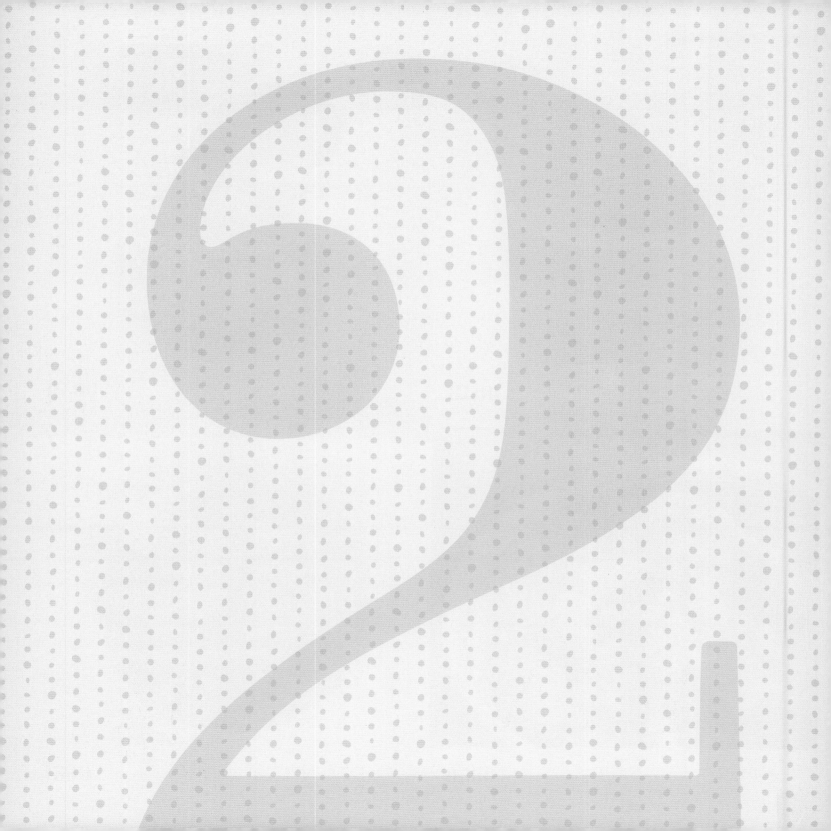

AU NATURAL

ORGANIC / ARTISAN / FRESH / PURE

NADINE SHAW
AUSTRALIA

0052

GRIP
USA
0053

SCOTT ERB AND DONNA DUFAULT
USA
0054

NADINE SHAW
AUSTRALIA
0055

HEATHER SPERLING
USA
0056

AZITA HOUSHIAR
USA

0057

MOLLY MCMAHON
USA

0058

AZITA HOUSHIAR

0059

MOLLY MCMAHON
USA

0060

REGAN BARONI
USA

0061

BERNADINE ROLNICKI
USA

0062

HEATHER SPERLING
USA

0063

HEATHER SPERLING
USA

0064

MOLLY MCMAHON
USA
0065

NICOLE ZARATE
USA
0066

HEATHER SPERLING
USA
0067

MICHELLE DEITER
USA
0068

MOLLY MCMAHON
USA

0069

GEORGIOS DETSIS
GREECE

0070

HEATHER SPERLING
USA

0071

CARLOS RIBEIRO
PORTUGAL

0072

MICHELLE DEITER
USA

0073

MOLLY MCMAHON
USA
0074

MOLLY MCMAHON
USA
0075

MOLLY MCMAHON
USA
0076

MOLLY MCMAHON
USA
0077

MOLLY MCMAHON
USA
0078

MOLLY MCMAHON
USA
0079

MOLLY MCMAHON
USA
0080

MOLLY MCMAHON
USA
0081

NICOLE ZARATE
USA
0082

KATE RIESENBERG
USA
0083

NADINE SHAW
AUSTRALIA
0084

KATE RIESENBERG
USA
0085

HEATHER SPERLING
USA
0086

JUSTIN B. PARIS
USA

ELISABETTA REDAELLI
ITALY

0088

SCOTT ERB AND DONNA DUFAULT
USA

0089

SCOTT ERB AND DONNA DUFAULT
USA

0090

GEORGIOS DETSIS
GREECE

0091

PARAGON MARKETING COMMUNICATIONS
KUWAIT

0092

TY LETTAU
USA

0093

GEORGIOS DETSIS
GREECE

0094

KATE RIESENBERG
USA

0095

GLOBAL

TRAVEL / IMPORTED / EXOTIC / ETHNIC / DIVERSE

GALDONES PHOTOGRAPHY
USA

0096

PARAGON MARKETING COMMUNICATIONS
KUWAIT

0097

HEATHER SPERLING
USA

0098

HEATHER SPERLING
USA

0099

HEATHER SPERLING
USA

0100

SHERI SILVER
USA **0101**

HEATHER SPERLING
USA **0102**

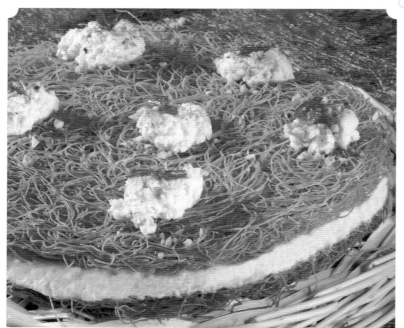

PARAGON MARKETING COMMUNICATIONS
KUWAIT **0103**

PARAGON MARKETING COMMUNICATIONS
KUWAIT **0104**

HEATHER SPERLING
USA

0105

JACQUI WEDEWER
USA

0106

HEATHER SPERLING
USA

0107

HEATHER SPERLING
USA

0108

DWAYNE KNIGHT
BARBADOS

0109

PARAGON MARKETING COMMUNICATIONS
KUWAIT
0110

PARAGON MARKETING COMMUNICATIONS
KUWAIT
0111

HEATHER SPERLING
USA
0112

PARAGON MARKETING COMMUNICATIONS
KUWAIT
0113

PARAGON MARKETING COMMUNICATIONS
KUWAIT
0114

PARAGON MARKETING COMMUNICATIONS
KUWAIT
0115

ANDREW HICKEY
USA
0116

KATE RIESENBERG
USA
0117

MOLLY MCMAHON
USA

0118

ERIC KLEINBERG
USA

0119

ANDREW HICKEY
USA

0120

BERNADINE ROLNICKI
USA

0121

PARAGON MARKETING
COMMUNICATIONS KUWAIT **0122**

ANDREW HICKEY
USA **0123**

ANDREW HICKEY
USA **0124**

PARAGON MARKETING
COMMUNICATIONS KUWAIT **0125**

PARAGON MARKETING
COMMUNICATIONS KUWAIT **0126**

PARAGON MARKETING
COMMUNICATIONS KUWAIT **0127**

PARAGON MARKETING
COMMUNICATIONS KUWAIT **0128**

MICHELLE DEITER
USA **0129**

PARAGON MARKETING
COMMUNICATIONS KUWAIT **0130**

berKsweLL

NEAL'S YARD DAIRY

this raw sheep's miLk cheese is made on the fLetcher famiLy's 6th gene-ration homestead near coventry. draining in coLanders gives the cheese its unusual shape. great miLk & extreme care give the cheese its fruity, nutey flavor.

GREAT BRITAIN $21.00/½#

appLe
ches

NEAL'S YARD DAIRY

the Last traditional made in England, the stein cows of the ap graze on grasses and mineral-rich shropshi which contributes to deep flavor, vegetaria

GREAT BRITAIN $14.5

HEATHER SPERLING
USA

0131

RACHEL DE MARTE
USA
0132

GALDONES PHOTOGRAPHY
USA
0133

GALDONES PHOTOGRAPHY
USA
0134

ELLIE MEYER
USA
0135

KATE RIESENBERG
USA

0136

AZITA HOUSHIAR
USA

0137

PARAGON MARKETING COMMUNICATIONS
KUWAIT

0138

KATE RIESENBERG
USA

0139

KATE RIESENBERG
USA

0140

KATE RIESENBERG
USA

0141

THAIN LIN TAY
SIGNAPORE

0142

THAIN LIN TAY
SIGNAPORE

0143

AZITA HOUSHIAR
USA
0144

ANDRES DANGOND
USA
0145

KATE RIESENBERG
USA
0146

HEATHER SPERLING
USA
0147

GEORGIOS DETSIS
GREECE
0148

PARAGON MARKETING
COMMUNICATIONS KUWAIT
0149

PARAGON MARKETING
COMMUNICATIONS KUWAIT
0150

PARAGON MARKETING
COMMUNICATIONS KUWAIT
0151

HEATHER SPERLING
USA
0152

ANDREW HICKEY
USA

0153

THAIN LIN TAY
SIGNAPORE
0154

TUAN H. BUI
USA
0155

GEORGIOS DETSIS
GREECE
0156

AZITA HOUSHIAR
USA
0157

SARA REMINGTON
USA

0158

GEORGIOS DETSIS
GREECE

0159

DWAYNE KNIGHT
BARBADOS

0160

BRIAN POREA
USA

0161

GALDONES PHOTOGRAPHY
USA

0162

GEORGIOS DETSIS
GREECE

0163

BRIAN POREA
USA

0164

ERIC KLEINBERG
USA

0165

KATE RIESENBERG
USA

0166

DENNIS LEE
USA
0167

GEORGIOS DETSIS
GREECE
0168

PARAGON MARKETING COMMUNICATIONS
KUWAIT
0169

DWAYNE KNIGHT
BARBADOS
0170

WATCH IT

SKINNY / CLEAN / LOW-CAL / LIGHT / SLIM

MOLLY MCMAHON
USA

0171

GALDONES PHOTOGRAPHY
USA
0172

PARAGON MARKETING
COMMUNICATIONS KUWAIT
0173

TY LETTAU
USA
0174

MOLLY MCMAHON
USA
0175

RONNIE SAINI
USA
0176

HEATHER SPERLING
USA
0177

HEATHER SPERLING
USA
0178

HEATHER SPERLING
USA
0179

ELISABETTA REDAELLI
ITALY
0180

MOLLY MCMAHON
USA

0181

MOLLY MCMAHON
USA

0182

BERNADINE ROLNICKI
USA

0183

BERNADINE ROLNICKI
USA

0184

ANDRES DANGOND
USA

0185

GEORGIOS DETSIS
GREECE

0186

KARI SKAFLEN
USA

0187

GEORGIOS DETSIS
GREECE

0188

THAIN LIN TAY
SIGNAPORE

0189

HEATHER SPERLING
USA

0190

BERNADINE ROLNICKI
USA

0191

CARA AND SCOTT NAVA
USA

0192

GEORGIOS DETSIS
GREECE
0193

KATE RIESENBERG
USA
0194

KATE RIESENBERG
USA
0195

KATE RIESENBERG
USA
0196

DENNIS LEE
USA
0197

LAUREN PODOLSKY
USA
0198

LAUREN PODOLSKY
USA
0199

MOLLY MCMAHON
USA
0200

HEATHER SPERLING
USA
0201

MARTA SASINOWSKA
USA

0202

HEATHER CROSBY
USA
0203

ERIC KLEINBERG
USA
0204

MICHELLE DEITER
USA
0205

NADINE SHAW
AUSTRALIA
0206

GRIP
USA

0207

KATE RIESENBERG
USA

0208

REGAN BARONI
USA

0209

PARAGON MARKETING COMMUNICATIONS
KUWAIT

0210

MOLLY MCMAHON
USA

0211

LAUREN PODOLSKY
USA

0212

PARAGON MARKETING COMMUNICATIONS
KUWAIT

0213

PARAGON MARKETING COMMUNICATIONS
KUWAIT

0214

PARAGON MARKETING COMMUNICATIONS **0215**
KUWAIT

RONNIE SAINI **0216**
USA

PARAGON MARKETING COMMUNICATIONS **0217**
KUWAIT

SCOTT ERB AND DONNA DUFAULT **0218**
USA

GLENN SCOTT
USA

0219

HEATHER SPERLING
USA

0220

HEATHER SPERLING
USA

0221

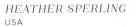

TUAN H. BUI
USA

0222

HEATHER SPERLING
USA

0223

TUAN H. BUI
USA

0224

HEATHER SPERLING
USA

0225

HEATHER SPERLING
USA

0226

SHERI SILVER
USA

0227

INDULGE

RICH / SWEET / SAVORY / GLAZED / FRIED

GRIP
USA

0228

NADINE SHAW
AUSTRALIA
0229

LAURA SANT
USA
0230

CARLOS RIBEIRO
PORTUGAL
0231

LAUREN PODOLSKY
USA
0232

HEATHER SPERLING
USA
0233

ELLIE MEYER
USA
0234

PARAGON MARKETING
COMMUNICATIONS KUWAIT
0235

PARAGON MARKETING
COMMUNICATIONS KUWAIT
0236

PARAGON MARKETING
COMMUNICATIONS KUWAIT
0237

TUAN H. BUI
USA
0242

JUSTIN B. PARIS
USA
0243

KATE RIESENBERG
USA
0244

GEORGIOS DETSIS
GREECE
0245

GEORGIOS DETSIS
GREECE
0246

GEORGIOS DETSIS
GREECE
0247

ANDREW HICKEY
USA
0248

ANDREW HICKEY
USA
0249

ANDREW HICKEY
USA
0250

JUSTIN B. PARIS
USA

0251

GALDONES PHOTOGRAPHY
USA
0252

MICHELLE DEITER
USA
0253

KATE RIESENBERG
USA
0254

NICOLE ZARATE
USA
0255

JUSTIN B. PARIS
USA

0256

GALDONES PHOTOGRAPHY
USA

0257

RUTH HUIMERIND
ESTONIA

0258

JUSTIN B. PARIS
USA

0259

PARAGON MARKETING COMMUNICATIONS
KUWAIT
0260

PARAGON MARKETING COMMUNICATIONS
KUWAIT
0261

PARAGON MARKETING COMMUNICATIONS
KUWAIT
0262

PARAGON MARKETING COMMUNICATIONS
KUWAIT
0263

CARA AND SCOTT NAVA
USA

0264

SHERI SILVER
USA

0265

ERIC KLEINBERG
USA

0266

MOLLY MCMAHON
USA

0267

NICOLE ZARATE
USA

0268

JUSTIN B. PARIS
USA

0269

ALYSA SLAY
USA

0270

SHERI SILVER
USA

0271

GALDONES PHOTOGRAPHY
USA

0272

MOLLY MCMAHON
USA

0273

TUAN H. BUI
USA

0274

TUAN H. BUI
USA

0275

GALDONES PHOTOGRAPHY
USA

0276

NADINE SHAW
AUSTRALIA

0277

HEATHER CROSBY
USA

0278

MOLLY MCMAHON
USA

0279

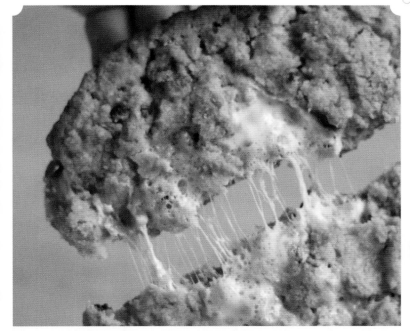

SHERI SILVER
USA

0280

MOLLY MCMAHON
USA

0281

GALDONES PHOTOGRAPHY
USA

0282

GALDONES PHOTOGRAPHY
USA

0283

ERIC KLEINBERG
USA

0284

PARAGON MARKETING COMMUNICATIONS
KUWAIT

0285

GALDONES PHOTOGRAPHY
USA

0286

GALDONES PHOTOGRAPHY
USA

0287

PARAGON MARKETING COMMUNICATIONS
KUWAIT

0288

GALDONES PHOTOGRAPHY
USA

0289

PARAGON MARKETING COMMUNICATIONS
KUWAIT

0299

PARAGON MARKETING COMMUNICATIONS
KUWAIT

0300

PARAGON MARKETING COMMUNICATIONS
KUWAIT

0301

PARAGON MARKETING COMMUNICATIONS
KUWAIT

0302

PARAGON MARKETING COMMUNICATIONS
KUWAIT

0303

PARAGON MARKETING COMMUNICATIONS
KUWAIT

0304

GRIP
USA

0305

MICHELLE DEITER
USA

0306

JUSTIN B. PARIS
USA

0307

DAVE BRADLEY
USA

SARA REMINGTON
USA

0309

GRIP
USA

0310

GRIP
USA

0311

PARAGON MARKETING COMMUNICATIONS
KUWAIT

0312

ERIC KLEINBERG
USA

0313

GRIP
USA

0314

DENNIS LEE
USA

0315

SHERI SILVER
USA

0316

0321

0322

0323

0324

PARAGON MARKETING COMMUNICATIONS
KUWAIT
0325

PARAGON MARKETING COMMUNICATIONS
KUWAIT
0326

PARAGON MARKETING COMMUNICATIONS
KUWAIT
0327

PARAGON MARKETING COMMUNICATIONS
KUWAIT
0328

GEORGIOS DETSIS
GREECE

0329

CARA AND SCOTT NAVA
USA

0330

CARA AND SCOTT NAVA
USA

0331

EZEQUIEL BECERRA
COSTA RICA

0332

KARI SKAFLEN
USA
0333

ANDREW HICKEY
USA
0334

KATE RIESENBERG
USA
0335

KATE RIESENBERG
USA
0336

ANTHONY TAHLIER
USA

0337

HEATHER SPERLING
USA
0338

HEATHER SPERLING
USA
0339

HEATHER SPERLING
USA
0340

HEATHER SPERLING
USA
0341

GRIP
USA
0346

TUAN H. BUI
USA
0347

GRIP
USA
0348

ANDREW HICKEY
USA
0349

GRIP

USA

0350

GEORGIOS DETSIS
USA
0351

CARA AND SCOTT NAVA
USA
0352

BRANDON FREITAS
USA
0353

ANDREW HICKEY
USA
0354

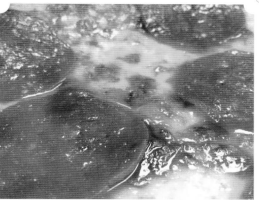

BRANDON FREITAS
USA
0355

BRANDON FREITAS
USA
0356

DENNIS LEE
USA
0357

GALDONES PHOTOGRAPHY
USA
0358

ELLIE MEYER
USA
0359

CHILL

REFRESH / QUENCH / FREEZE

SARA REMINGTON
USA

0360

PARAGON MARKETING COMMUNICATIONS KUWAIT **0361**

HEATHER SPERLING USA **0362**

PARAGON MARKETING COMMUNICATIONS KUWAIT **0363**

BRANDON FREITAS USA **0364**

PARAGON MARKETING COMMUNICATIONS KUWAIT **0365**

KATE RIESENBERG USA **0366**

PARAGON MARKETING COMMUNICATIONS KUWAIT **0367**

TY LETTAU USA **0368**

PARAGON MARKETING COMMUNICATIONS KUWAIT **0369**

ANTHONY TAHLIER
USA

0370

GALDONES PHOTOGRAPHY
USA

0371

ERIC KLEINBERG
USA

0372

ERIC KLEINBERG
USA

0373

CARA AND SCOTT NAVA
USA

0374

TUAN H. BUI
USA

0375

HEATHER SPERLING
USA

0376

TUAN H. BUI
USA

0377

ANTHONY TAHLIER
USA

0378

KARI SKAFLEN
USA

0379

HEATHER SPERLING
USA

0380

MICHELLE DEITER
USA

0381

ERIC KLEINBERG
USA

0382

ANTHONY TAHLIER
USA

0383

PARAGON MARKETING COMMUNICATIONS
KUWAIT

0384

ANTHONY TAHLIER
USA

0385

PARAGON MARKETING COMMUNICATIONS
KUWAIT

0386

PARAGON MARKETING COMMUNICATIONS
KUWAIT

0387

PARAGON MARKETING COMMUNICATIONS
KUWAIT **0388**

PARAGON MARKETING COMMUNICATIONS
KUWAIT **0389**

PARAGON MARKETING COMMUNICATIONS
KUWAIT **0390**

PARAGON MARKETING COMMUNICATIONS
KUWAIT **0391**

HEATHER SPERLING
USA
0392

SHERI SILVER
USA
0393

HEATHER SPERLING
USA
0394

PARAGON MARKETING COMMUNICATIONS
USA
0395

ERIC KLEINBERG
USA

0396

GALDONES PHOTOGRAPHY
USA
0397

PARAGON MARKETING
COMMUNICATIONS KUWAIT
0398

PARAGON MARKETING
COMMUNICATIONS KUWAIT
0399

PARAGON MARKETING
COMMUNICATIONS KUWAIT
0400

PARAGON MARKETING
COMMUNICATIONS KUWAIT
0401

PARAGON MARKETING
COMMUNICATIONS KUWAIT
0402

GALDONES PHOTOGRAPHY
USA
0403

PARAGON MARKETING
COMMUNICATIONS KUWAIT
0404

GALDONES PHOTOGRAPHY
USA
0405

HEAT

SPICY / FIERY / SMOKY / ZESTY / STEAMY

JUSTIN B. PARIS
USA

0406

PARAGON MARKETING COMMUNICATIONS **0407**
KUWAIT

HEATHER SPERLING **0408**
USA

HEATHER SPERLING **0409**
USA

HEATHER SPERLING **0410**
USA

ANTHONY TAHLIER
USA

0411

PARAGON MARKETING COMMUNICATIONS
KUWAIT

0412

ANTHONY TAHLIER
USA

0443

SCOTT ERB AND DONNA DUFAULT
USA

0444

ELISABETTA REDAELLI
ITALY

0415

MOLLY MCMAHON
USA

0416

MOLLY MCMAHON
USA

0417

PARAGON MARKETING COMMUNICATIONS
KUWAIT

0418

MICHELLE DEITER
USA

0449

CARA AND SCOTT NAVA
USA

0420

ANDREW HICKEY
USA

0421

BRIAN POREA
USA

0422

NICOLE ZARATE
USA

0423

NADINE SHAW
AUSTRALIA

0424

SHERI SILVER
USA
0425

PARAGON MARKETING COMMUNICATIONS
KUWAIT
0426

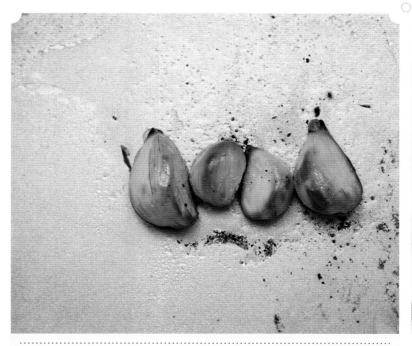

MOLLY MCMAHON
USA
0427

HEATHER SPERLING
USA
0428

GLENN SCOTT
USA

0429

GLENN SCOTT
USA

0430

PARAGON MARKETING COMMUNICATIONS
KUWAIT

0431

DENNIS LEE
USA

0432

GLENN SCOTT
USA

0433

MOLLY MCMAHON
USA

0434

PARAGON MARKETING COMMUNICATIONS
KUWAIT

0435

ANTHONY TAHLIER
USA

0436

MICHELLE DEITER
USA

0437

PARAGON MARKETING COMMUNICATIONS
KUWAIT

0438

BRANDON FREITAS
USA
0439

PARAGON MARKETING COMMUNICATIONS
KUWAIT
0440

BRANDON FREITAS
USA
0441

BRANDON FREITAS
USA
0442

GRIP
USA

0443

GALDONES PHOTOGRAPHY
USA

0444

GALDONES PHOTOGRAPHY
USA

0445

GRIP
USA

0446

WET

BUBBLY / REFRESHING / FIZZY / TART / SMOOTH

GRIP
USA

0447

GRIP
USA

0448

GRIP
USA

0449

GEORGIOS DETSIS
GREECE

0450

ERIC KLEINBERG
USA

0451

GALDONES PHOTOGRAPHY
USA

0452

GALDONES PHOTOGRAPHY
USA

0453

GALDONES PHOTOGRAPHY
USA

0454

GALDONES PHOTOGRAPHY
USA

0455

0456

0457

0458

0459

RUTH HUIMERIND
ESTONIA

0460

DWAYNE KNIGHT
BARBADOS

0461

RUTH HUIMERIND
ESTONIA

0462

GALDONES PHOTOGRAPHY
USA

0463

TUAN H. BUI
USA

0464

HEATHER SPERLING
USA

0465

ANDREW HICKEY
USA

0466

SCOTT ERB AND DONNA DUFAULT
USA

0467

ERIC KLEINBERG
USA

0468

ERIC KLEINBERG
USA

0469

REGAN BARONI
USA

0470

SCOTT ERB AND DONNA DUFAULT
USA

0471

GRIP
USA

0472

GRIP
USA

0477

ERIC KLEINBERG
USA

0478

KATE RIESENBERG
USA

0479

KARI SKAFLEN
USA

0480

RACHEL DE MARTE
USA

0481

PARAGON MARKETING COMMUNICATIONS
KUWAIT

0482

PARAGON MARKETING COMMUNICATIONS
KUWAIT

0483

GALDONES PHOTOGRAPHY
USA

0484

ERIC KLEINBERG
USA

0485

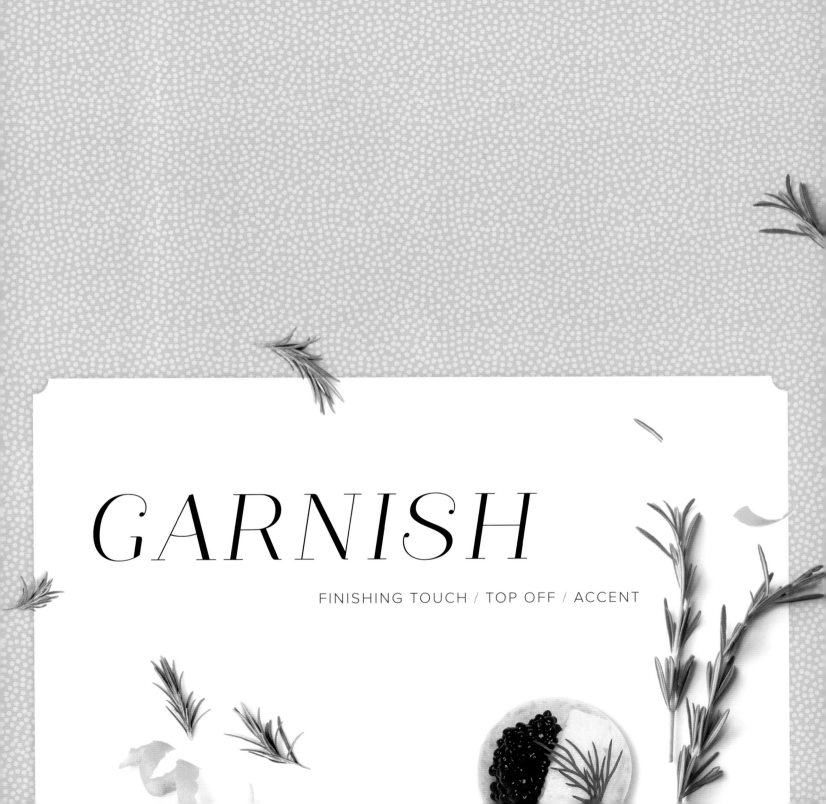

GARNISH

FINISHING TOUCH / TOP OFF / ACCENT

ANTHONY TAHLIER
USA

0486

GALDONES PHOTOGRAPHY
USA

0487

ANDRES DANGOND
USA

0488

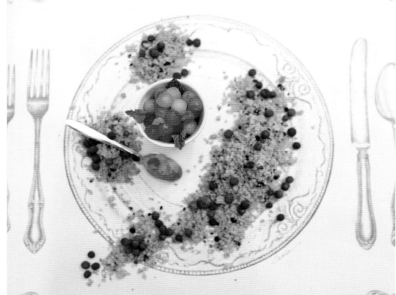

HEATHER SPERLING
USA

0489

GALDONES PHOTOGRAPHY
USA

0490

GALDONES PHOTOGRAPHY
USA

0491

GALDONES PHOTOGRAPHY
USA

0492

GALDONES PHOTOGRAPHY
USA

0493

GALDONES PHOTOGRAPHY
USA

0494

HEATHER SPERLING
USA
0495

BERNADINE ROLNICKI
USA
0496

LUKASZ FUKS
POLAND
0497

KARI SKAFLEN
USA
0498

KATE RIESENBERG
USA
0499

PARAGON MARKETING
COMMUNICATIONS KUWAIT
0500

GEORGIOS DETSIS
GREECE
0501

HEATHER SPERLING
USA
0502

GEORGIOS DETSIS
GREECE
0503

JACQUI WEDEWER
USA

0504

KARI SKAFLEN
USA

0505

ELLIE MEYER
USA

0506

GEORGIOS DETSIS
GREECE

0507

GEORGIOS DETSIS
GREECE

0508

GALDONES PHOTOGRAPHY
USA

0509

DWAYNE KNIGHT
BARBADOS

0510

CARA AND SCOTT NAVA
USA

0511

NICOLE ZARATE
USA
0512

MICHELLE DEITER
USA
0513

NADINE SHAW
AUSTRALIA
0514

HEATHER SPERLING
USA
0515

LAURA SANT
USA

0516

MOLLY MCMAHON
USA

0517

GALDONES PHOTOGRAPHY
USA

0518

KATE RIESENBERG
USA

0519

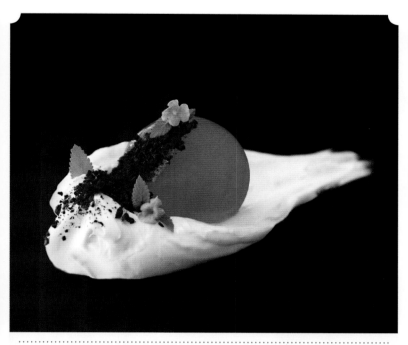

ANDRES DANGOND
USA

0521

CARA AND SCOTT NAVA
USA

0522

TY LETTAU
USA

0523

TUAN H. BUI
USA

0524

*PARAGON MARKETING
COMMUNICATIONS* KUWAIT **0525**

*PARAGON MARKETING
COMMUNICATIONS* KUWAIT **0526**

*PARAGON MARKETING
COMMUNICATIONS* KUWAIT **0527**

TUAN H. BUI
USA **0528**

TUAN H. BUI
USA **0529**

TUAN H. BUI
USA **0530**

TUAN H. BUI
USA **0531**

TUAN H. BUI
USA **0532**

TUAN H. BUI
USA **0533**

TUAN H. BUI
USA
0534

CARA AND SCOTT NAVA
USA
0535

HEATHER SPERLING
USA
0536

ERIC KLEINBERG
USA
0537

BRIAN POREA
USA
0538

PARAGON MARKETING COMMUNICATIONS
KUWAIT
0539

MOLLY MCMAHON
USA
0540

MICHELLE DEITER
USA
0541

SCOTT ERB AND DONNA DUFAULT
USA

0542

GALDONES PHOTOGRAPHY
USA

0543

GALDONES PHOTOGRAPHY
USA

0544

GALDONES PHOTOGRAPHY
USA

0545

HEATHER SPERLING
USA

0546

GALDONES PHOTOGRAPHY
USA
0547

GALDONES PHOTOGRAPHY
USA
0548

GALDONES PHOTOGRAPHY
USA
0549

GALDONES PHOTOGRAPHY
USA
0550

GRIP
USA

0551

MOLLY MCMAHON
USA

0552

NADINE SHAW
AUSTRALIA

0553

ANDREW HICKEY
USA

0554

PARAGON MARKETING COMMUNICATIONS
KUWAIT

0555

GALDONES PHOTOGRAPHY
USA

0560

GALDONES PHOTOGRAPHY
USA

0561

HEATHER SPERLING
USA

0562

GALDONES PHOTOGRAPHY
USA

0563

0565

0566

0567

0568

GALDONES PHOTOGRAPHY
USA

0569

GALDONES PHOTOGRAPHY
USA

0570

GALDONES PHOTOGRAPHY
USA

0571

GALDONES PHOTOGRAPHY
USA

0572

GALDONES PHOTOGRAPHY
USA

0573

GALDONES PHOTOGRAPHY
USA

0574

GALDONES PHOTOGRAPHY
USA

0575

GALDONES PHOTOGRAPHY
USA

0576

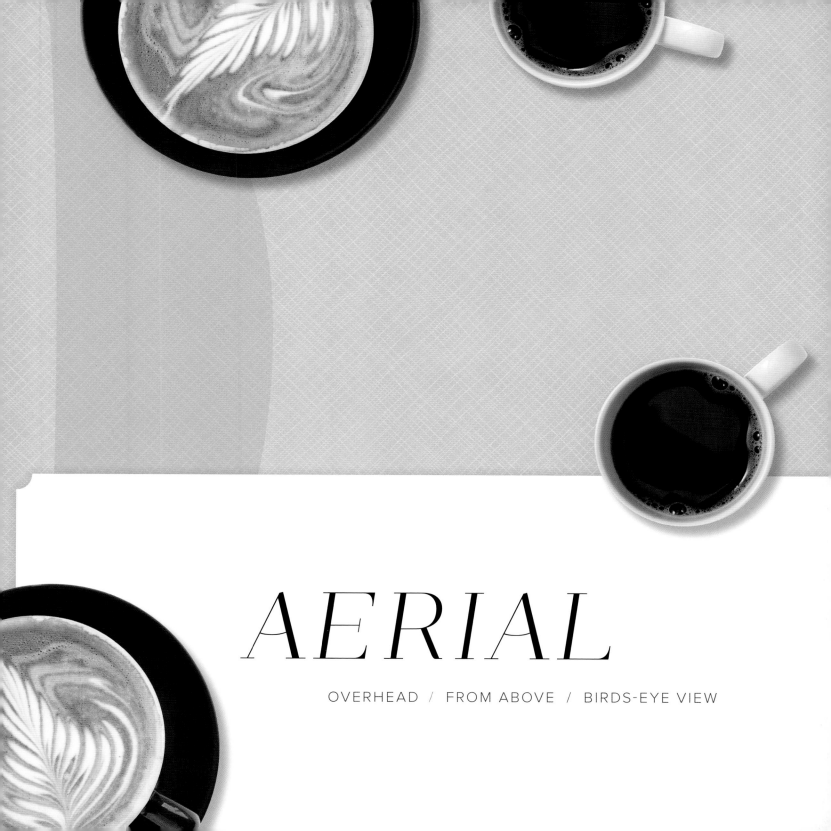

AERIAL

OVERHEAD / FROM ABOVE / BIRDS-EYE VIEW

JUSTIN B. PARIS
USA

JUSTIN B. PARIS
USA
0578

TUAN H. BUI
USA
0579

NADINE SHAW
AUSTRALIA
0580

MOLLY MCMAHON
USA
0581

AZITA HOUSHIAR
USA
0582

MOLLY MCMAHON
USA
0583

TUAN H. BUI
USA
0584

TY LETTAU
USA
0585

MOLLY MCMAHON
USA
0586

KATE RIESENBERG
USA
0587

AZITA HOUSHIAR
USA
0588

NADINE SHAW
AUSTRALIA
0589

TY LETTAU
USA
0590

LISA ALLEN LAMBERT
USA

0591

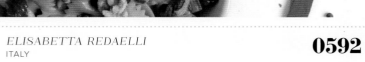

ELISABETTA REDAELLI
ITALY

0592

ANTHONY TAHLIER
USA

0593

NADINE SHAW
AUSTRALIA

0594

TUAN H. BUI
USA **0595**

ERIC KLEINBERG
USA **0596**

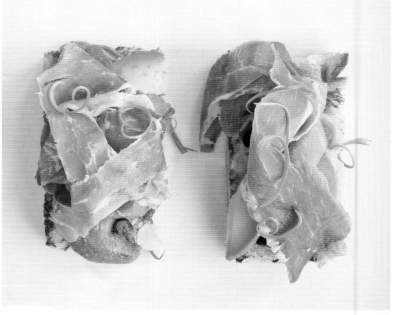

TUAN H. BUI
USA **0597**

GALDONES PHOTOGRAPHY
USA **0598**

TUAN H. BUI
USA

0599

ERIC KLEINBERG
USA

0604

GRIP
USA

0605

DENNIS LEE
USA

0606

JUSTIN B. PARIS
USA

0607

ERIC KLEINBERG
USA

0608

ARI BENDERSKY
USA

0609

CARLOS RIBEIRO
PORTUGAL

0610

MOLLY MCMAHON
USA

0611

GALDONES PHOTOGRAPHY
USA

0612

GALDONES PHOTOGRAPHY
USA

0613

arob

BORIS LJUBICIC
CROATIA
0614

BORIS LJUBICIC
CROATIA
0615

BORIS LJUBICIC
CROATIA
0616

nge

BORIS LJUBICIC
CROATIA
0617

BORIS LJUBICIC
CROATIA
0618

BORIS LJUBICIC
CROATIA
0619

BRANDON FREITAS
USA
0620

ANTHONY TAHLIER
USA
0621

ANTHONY TAHLIER
USA
0622

SCOTT ERB AND DONNA DUFAULT
USA
0623

ANTHONY TAHLIER
USA
0624

MOLLY MCMAHON
USA
0625

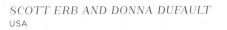

HEATHER SPERLING
USA
0626

LUKASZ FUKS
POLAND

0627

NADINE SHAW
AUSTRALIA

0628

MOLLY MCMAHON
USA

0629

RENATO SEALY
BARBADOS, W.I.

0630

HEATHER VAN GAALE
USA

0631

ANTHONY TAHLIER
USA
0632

ANTHONY TAHLIER
USA
0633

ALYSA SLAY
USA
0634

ANTHONY TAHLIER
USA
0635

SHERI SILVER
USA
0636

HEATHER VAN GAALE
USA
0637

HEATHER VAN GAALE
USA
0638

SHERI SILVER
USA
0639

DENNIS LEE
USA

0640

MOLLY MCMAHON
USA

0641

MARTA SASINOWSKA
USA

0642

NICOLE ZARATE
USA

0643

GALDONES PHOTOGRAPHY
USA **0644**

GALDONES PHOTOGRAPHY
USA **0645**

ERIC KLEINBERG
USA **0646**

GALDONES PHOTOGRAPHY
USA **0647**

GALDONES PHOTOGRAPHY
USA

0648

GALDONES PHOTOGRAPHY
USA

0649

GALDONES PHOTOGRAPHY
USA

0650

GALDONES PHOTOGRAPHY
USA

0651

NARRATIVE

SCENE / MOOD / TALE / CONTEXT / STAGE

MARTA SASINOWSKA
USA

0652

MARTA SASINOWSKA
USA

0653

MARTA SASINOWSKA
USA

0654

MOLLY MCMAHON
USA

0655

GALDONES PHOTOGRAPHY
USA

0656

TUAN H. BUI
USA
0657

NANDY VILLONGCO
USA
0658

TUAN H. BUI
USA
0659

TUAN H. BUI
USA
0660

GEORGIOS DETSIS
GREECE
0661

GEORGIOS DETSIS
GREECE
0662

GEORGIOS DETSIS
GREECE
0663

BERNADINE ROLNICKI
USA
0664

KATE RIESENBERG
USA
0665

TUAN H. BUI
USA
0666

ELISABETTA REDAELLI
ITALY
0667

GEORGIOS DETSIS
GREECE
0668

CARA AND SCOTT NAVA
USA
0669

GALDONES PHOTOGRAPHY
USA

0670

GRIP
USA
0671

CARA AND SCOTT NAVA
USA
0672

SHERI SILVER
USA
0673

SHERI SILVER
USA
0674

NADINE SHAW
AUSTRALIA
0675

ARI BENDERSKY
USA
0676

ARI BENDERSKY
USA
0677

RACHEL DE MARTE
USA
0678

AZITA HOUSHIAR
USA
0679

ELLIE MEYER
USA
0680

GEORGIOS DETSIS
GREECE
0681

PARAGON MARKETING
COMMUNICATIONS KUWAIT
0682

BRIAN POREA
USA
0683

the
SAUTÉ

Net Wt. 16 oz {454g}

THE
flavor
by
STEPHANIE IZARD

GRIP
USA

0685

GRIP
USA

0686

TUAN H. BUI
USA

0687

RACHEL DE MARTE
USA

0688

DAVID ROBERT ELLIOTT
USA
0689

DAVID ROBERT ELLIOTT
USA
0690

DAVID ROBERT ELLIOTT
USA
0691

DAVID ROBERT ELLIOTT
USA
0692

DENNIS LEE
USA

0693

DENNIS LEE
USA

0694

DENNIS LEE
USA

0695

DENNIS LEE
USA

0696

KATE RIESENBERG
USA

0697

ANTHONY TAHLIER
USA

0698

ERIC KLEINBERG
USA

0699

KATE RIESENBERG
USA

0700

GALDONES PHOTOGRAPHY
USA

0701

GALDONES PHOTOGRAPHY
USA

0702

ERIC KLEINBERG
USA

0703

GRIP
USA

0704

BRANDON FREITAS
USA

0705

MOLLY MCMAHON
USA

0706

MOLLY MCMAHON
USA

0707

KATE RIESENBERG
USA

0708

ANDREW HICKEY
USA

0709

SHERI SILVER
USA

0710

ANDREW HICKEY
USA

0711

DENNIS LEE
USA

0712

ANDREW HICKEY
USA

0713

NADINE SHAW
AUSTRALIA

0714

NADINE SHAW
AUSTRALIA

0715

ROOT STUDIO
ENGLAND

0716

ROOT STUDIO
ENGLAND

0717

ROOT STUDIO
ENGLAND

0718

PARAGON MARKETING COMMUNICATIONS
KUWAIT
0719

ARI BENDERSKY
USA
0720

PARAGON MARKETING COMMUNICATIONS
KUWAIT
0721

PARAGON MARKETING COMMUNICATIONS
KUWAIT
0722

PARAGON MARKETING COMMUNICATIONS
KUWAIT

0723

PARAGON MARKETING COMMUNICATIONS
KUWAIT

0724

PARAGON MARKETING COMMUNICATIONS
KUWAIT

0725

PARAGON MARKETING COMMUNICATIONS
KUWAIT

0726

GRIP
USA
0727

GRIP
USA
0728

ARI BENDERSKY
USA
0729

KATE RIESENBERG
USA
0730

PARAGON MARKETING
COMMUNICATIONS KUWAIT **0731**

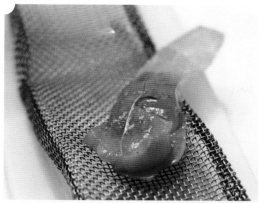

HEATHER SPERLING
USA **0732**

PARAGON MARKETING
COMMUNICATIONS KUWAIT **0733**

TUAN H. BUI
USA **0734**

ANTHONY TAHLIER
USA **0735**

PARAGON MARKETING
COMMUNICATIONS KUWAIT **0736**

RUTH HUIMERIND
ESTONIA **0737**

RUTH HUIMERIND
ESTONIA **0738**

PARAGON MARKETING
COMMUNICATIONS KUWAIT **0739**

LUKASZ FUKS
POLAND
0740

LUKASZ FUKS
POLAND
0741

LUKASZ FUKS
POLAND
0742

ALLAN PENN
USA
0743

ALLAN PENN
USA

0744

ALLAN PENN
USA

0745

ALLAN PENN
USA

0746

ALLAN PENN
USA

0747

HEATHER VAN GAALE

USA

0748

HEATHER SPERLING
USA
0749

HEATHER SPERLING
USA
0750

KATE RIESENBERG
USA
0751

GRIP
USA
0752

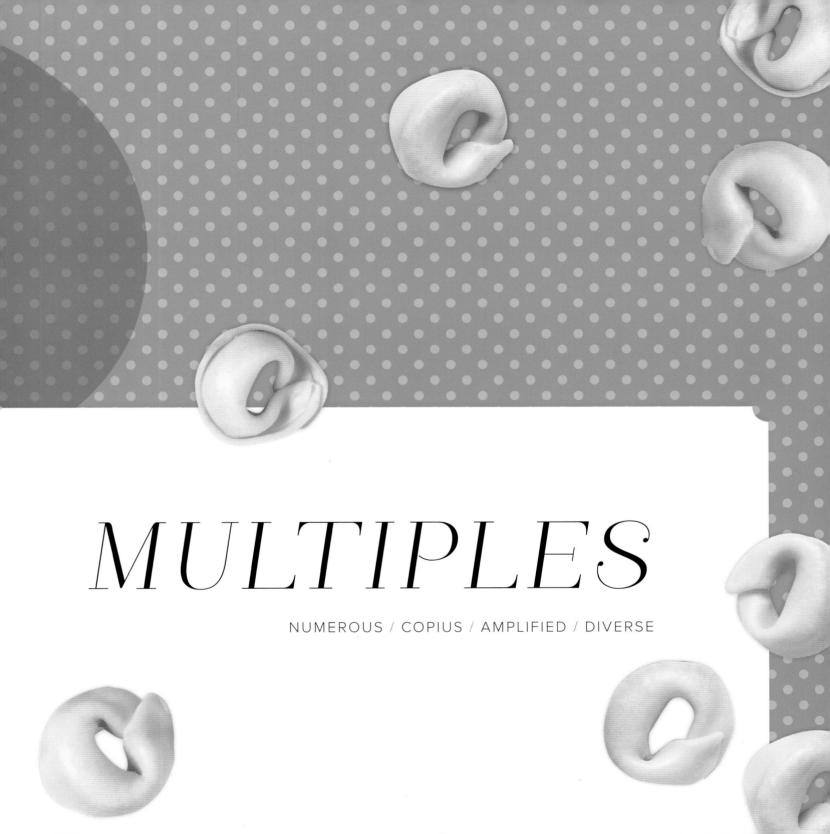

MULTIPLES

NUMEROUS / COPIUS / AMPLIFIED / DIVERSE

JUSTIN B. PARIS
USA

0753

GALDONES PHOTOGRAPHY
USA
0754

GALDONES PHOTOGRAPHY
USA
0755

GALDONES PHOTOGRAPHY
USA
0756

SCOTT ERB AND DONNA DUFAULT
USA
0757

TUAN H. BUI
USA

0758

TUAN H. BUI
USA

0759

TUAN H. BUI
USA

0760

NANDY VILLONGCO
USA

0761

GRIP
USA

0762

GALDONES PHOTOGRAPHY
USA

0763

GEORGIOS DETSIS
GREECE

0764

ELISABETTA REDAELLI
ITALY

0765

BERNADINE ROLNICKI
USA

0766

TUAN H. BUI
USA

0767

ELISABETTA REDAELLI
ITALY

0768

MOLLY MCMAHON
USA

0769

SCOTT ERB AND DONNA DUFAULT
USA

0770

GALDONES PHOTOGRAPHY
USA

0771

GALDONES PHOTOGRAPHY
USA
0772

MOLLY MCMAHON
USA
0773

GEORGIOS DETSIS
GREECE
0774

GALDONES PHOTOGRAPHY
USA
0775

GLENN SCOTT
USA

0776

BRIAN POREA
USA

0777

GALDONES PHOTOGRAPHY
USA

0778

GEORGIOS DETSIS
GREECE

0779

GALDONES PHOTOGRAPHY
USA

0780

DENNIS LEE
USA
0781

DENNIS LEE
USA
0782

AZITA HOUSHIAR
USA
0783

CARA AND SCOTT NAVA
USA
0784

ELLIE MEYER
USA
0785

KATE RIESENBERG
USA
0786

BRIAN POREA
USA
0787

AZITA HOUSHIAR
USA
0788

PARAGON MARKETING
COMMUNICATIONS KUWAIT
0789

CARA AND SCOTT NAVA
USA

0790

BRIAN POREA
USA

0791

GRIP
USA

0792

DENNIS LEE
USA

0793

PARAGON MARKETING COMMUNICATIONS
KUWAIT

0794

KATE RIESENBERG
USA

0795

KATE RIESENBERG
USA

0796

KATE RIESENBERG
USA

0797

KATE RIESENBERG
USA

0798

KATE RIESENBERG
USA

0799

ANDREW HICKEY
USA

0800

PARAGON MARKETING COMMUNICATIONS
KUWAIT

0801

MICHELLE DEITER
USA

0802

MICHELLE DEITER
USA

0803

GALDONES PHOTOGRAPHY
USA

0804

ANDREW HICKEY
USA

0805

NADINE SHAW
AUSTRALIA

0806

ANDREW HICKEY
USA

0807

ANDREW HICKEY
USA

0808

ANDREW HICKEY
USA

0809

CARA AND SCOTT NAVA
USA

0810

ANDREW HICKEY
USA

0811

PARAGON MARKETING COMMUNICATIONS
KUWAIT

0812

PARAGON MARKETING COMMUNICATIONS
KUWAIT

0813

RACHEL DE MARTE
USA

0814

MOLLY MCMAHON

USA

0815

ERIC KLEINBERG
USA

0816

ERIC KLEINBERG
USA

0817

PARAGON MARKETING COMMUNICATIONS
KUWAIT

0818

PARAGON MARKETING COMMUNICATIONS
KUWAIT

0819

MOLLY MCMAHON
USA

0820

MOLLY MCMAHON
USA

0821

PARAGON MARKETING COMMUNICATIONS
KUWAIT

0822

PARAGON MARKETING COMMUNICATIONS
KUWAIT

0823

ANDREW HICKEY
USA
0824

PARAGON MARKETING COMMUNICATIONS
KUWAIT
0825

PARAGON MARKETING COMMUNICATIONS
KUWAIT
0826

PARAGON MARKETING COMMUNICATIONS
KUWAIT
0827

PARAGON MARKETING COMMUNICATIONS
KUWAIT **0828**

PARAGON MARKETING COMMUNICATIONS
KUWAIT **0829**

PARAGON MARKETING COMMUNICATIONS
KUWAIT **0830**

PARAGON MARKETING COMMUNICATIONS
KUWAIT **0831**

PARAGON MARKETING COMMUNICATIONS
KUWAIT **0832**

PARAGON MARKETING COMMUNICATIONS
KUWAIT **0833**

PARAGON MARKETING COMMUNICATIONS
KUWAIT **0834**

PARAGON MARKETING COMMUNICATIONS
KUWAIT **0835**

PARAGON MARKETING COMMUNICATIONS
KUWAIT
0836

ELISABETTA REDAELLI
ITALY
0837

PARAGON MARKETING COMMUNICATIONS
KUWAIT
0838

PARAGON MARKETING COMMUNICATIONS
KUWAIT
0839

HEATHER VAN GAALE
USA

0840

ANTHONY TAHLIER
USA

0841

SHERI SILVER
USA

0842

HEATHER SPERLING
USA

0843

ANTHONY TAHLIER
USA

0844

SHERI SILVER
USA

0845

HEATHER SPERLING
USA
0846

HEATHER SPERLING
USA
0847

HEATHER SPERLING
USA
0848

SHERI SILVER
USA
0849

TY LETTAU
USA

0850

HEATHER VAN GAALE
USA

0851

HEATHER VAN GAALE
USA

0852

SHERI SILVER
USA

0853

TY LETTAU
USA

0854

ARI BENDERSKY
USA

0855

ARI BENDERSKY
USA

0856

ARI BENDERSKY
USA

0857

LUKASZ FUKS
POLAND
0858

RONNIE SAINI
USA
0859

KATE RIESENBERG
USA
0860

HEATHER SPERLING
USA
0861

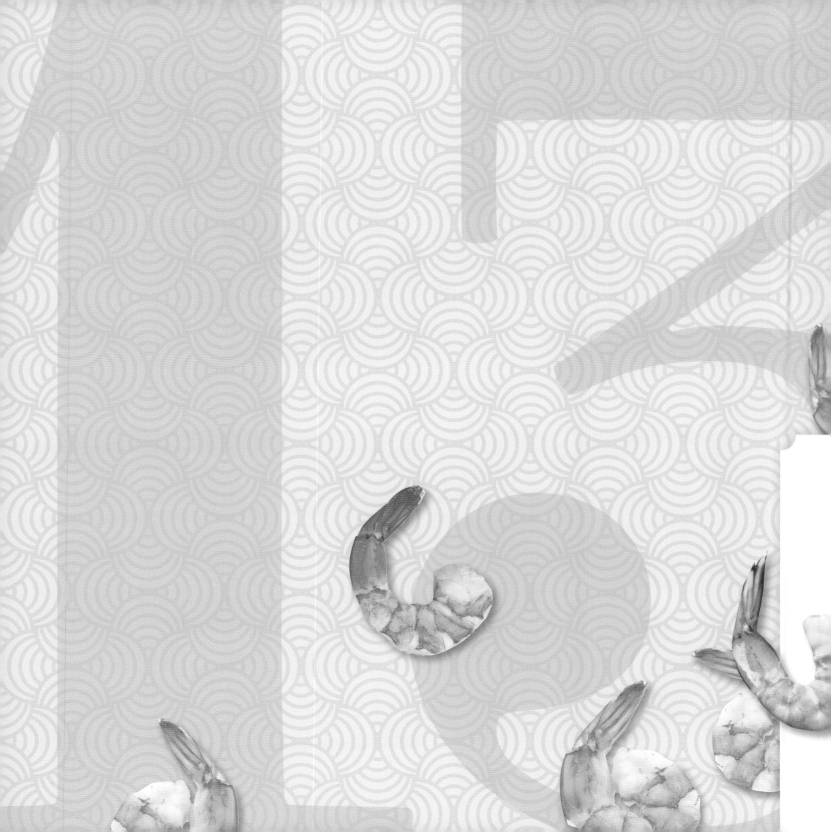

SEA

DELICATE / POACHED / WILD-CAUGHT / SMOKED

SCOTT ERB AND DONNA DUFAULT
USA

0862

ARI BENDERSKY
USA

0863

KARI SKAFLEN
USA

0864

ARI BENDERSKY
USA

0865

ANDREW HICKEY
USA

0866

KATE RIESENBERG
USA

0867

SCOTT ERB AND DONNA
DUFAULT USA

0868

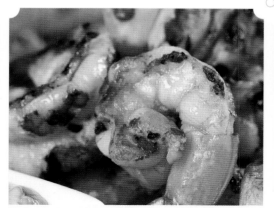

PARAGON MARKETING
COMMUNICATIONS KUWAIT

0869

PARAGON MARKETING
COMMUNICATIONS KUWAIT

0870

ALLAN PENN
USA

0871

GLENN SCOTT
USA

0872

SCOTT ERB AND DONNA DUFAULT
USA

0873

ELLIE MEYER
USA

0874

TUAN H. BUI
USA

0875

KATE RIESENBERG
USA

0876

CARA AND SCOTT NAVA
USA

0877

THAIN LIN TAY
SINGAPORE

0878

CARA AND SCOTT NAVA
USA

0879

TUAN H. BUI
USA

0880

TUAN H. BUI
USA
0881

ERIC KLEINBERG
USA
0882

HEATHER SPERLING
USA
0883

RACHEL DE MARTE
USA
0884

PARAGON MARKETING COMMUNICATIONS
KUWAIT
0885

PARAGON MARKETING COMMUNICATIONS
KUWAIT
0886

CARA AND SCOTT NAVA
USA
0887

PARAGON MARKETING COMMUNICATIONS
KUWAIT
0888

PARAGON MARKETING COMMUNICATIONS
KUWAIT

0889

ERIC KLEINBERG
USA

0890

PARAGON MARKETING COMMUNICATIONS
KUWAIT

0891

HEATHER SPERLING
USA

0892

DAVE BRADLEY
USA

0893

TUAN H. BUI
USA

0894

GALDONES PHOTOGRAPHY
USA

0895

GALDONES PHOTOGRAPHY
USA

0896

SCOTT ERB AND DONNA DUFAULT
USA

0897

0898

0899

0900

0901

HEATHER SPERLING
USA
0902

HEATHER SPERLING
USA
0903

HEATHER SPERLING
USA
0904

HEATHER SPERLING
USA
0905

ANDRES DANGOND
USA
0906

SHERI SILVER
USA
0907

HEATHER SPERLING
USA
0908

ANDRES DANGOND
USA
0909

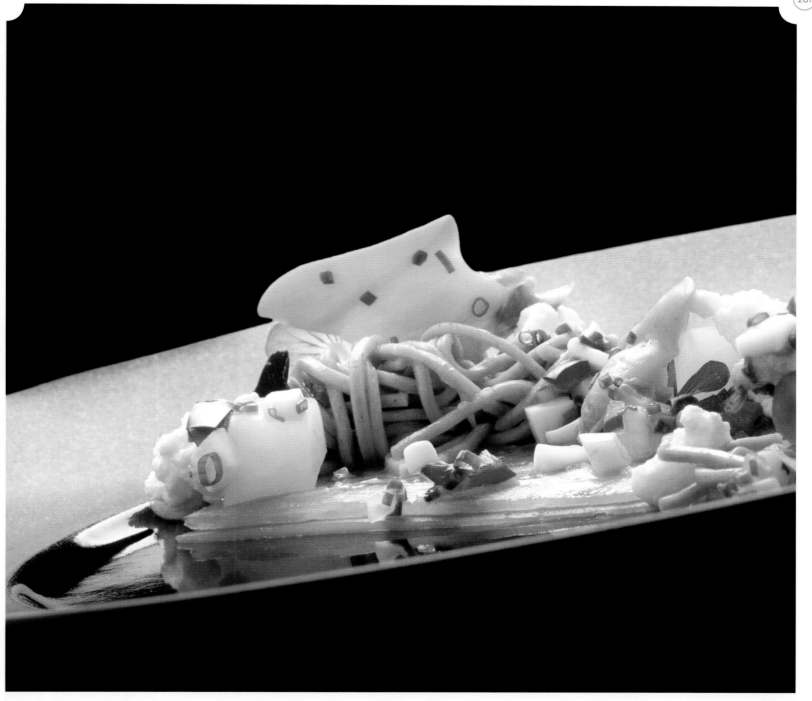

ERIC KLEINBERG
USA

0910

ERIC KLEINBERG
USA

0911

RACHEL DE MARTE
USA

0912

REGAN BARONI
USA

0913

ERIC KLEINBERG
USA

0914

MOLLY MCMAHON
USA

0915

GALDONES PHOTOGRAPHY
USA

0916

GALDONES PHOTOGRAPHY
USA

0917

GALDONES PHOTOGRAPHY
USA

0918

CARA AND SCOTT NAVA
USA

0919

GALDONES PHOTOGRAPHY
USA

0920

GALDONES PHOTOGRAPHY
USA

0921

GALDONES PHOTOGRAPHY
USA

0922

CARA AND SCOTT NAVA
USA

0923

ANTHONY TAHLIER
USA

0924

HEATHER SPERLING
USA
0925

ERIC KLEINBERG
USA
0926

GALDONES PHOTOGRAPHY
USA
0927

ERIC KLEINBERG
USA
0928

ERIC KLEINBERG
USA

0929

GALDONES PHOTOGRAPHY
USA

0930

GRIP
USA

0931

ERIC KLEINBERG
USA

0932

GALDONES PHOTOGRAPHY
USA

0933

GALDONES PHOTOGRAPHY
USA

0934

ERIC KLEINBERG
USA

0935

ERIC KLEINBERG
USA

0936

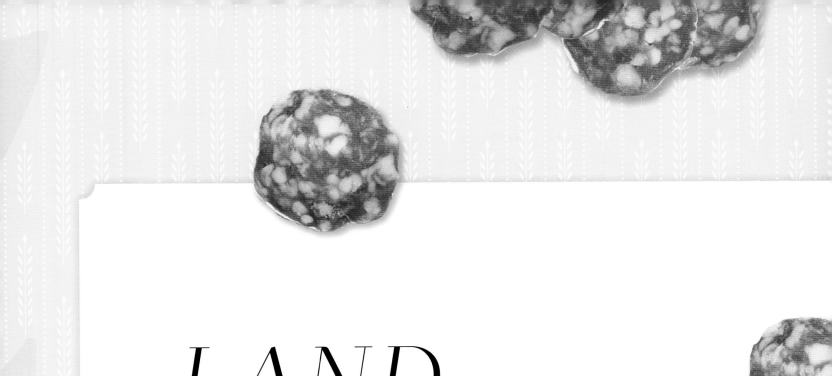

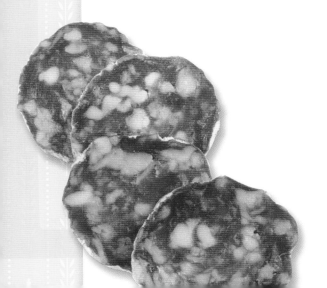

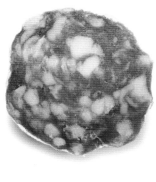

LAND

GRILLED / CURED / SEARED / ROASTED

GLENN SCOTT
USA

0937

ELLIE MEYER
USA

0938

PARAGON MARKETING COMMUNICATIONS
KUWAIT

0939

HEATHER SPERLING
USA

0940

PARAGON MARKETING COMMUNICATIONS
KUWAIT

0941

GRIP
USA

0942

ERIC KLEINBERG
USA

0943

ERIC KLEINBERG
USA

0944

GALDONES PHOTOGRAPHY
USA

0945

GALDONES PHOTOGRAPHY
USA

0946

GALDONES PHOTOGRAPHY
USA

0947

GALDONES PHOTOGRAPHY

0948

GALDONES PHOTOGRAPHY
USA

0949

GLENN SCOTT
USA

0950

PARAGON MARKETING COMMUNICATIONS KUWAIT **0951**

JACQUI WEDEWER
USA **0952**

HEATHER SPERLING
USA **0953**

HEATHER SPERLING
USA **0954**

ANDREW HICKEY
USA **0955**

RACHEL DE MARTE
USA **0956**

ANDREW HICKEY
USA **0957**

RACHEL DE MARTE
USA **0958**

PARAGON MARKETING COMMUNICATIONS KUWAIT **0959**

JACQUI WEDEWER
USA
0960

TY LETTAU
USA
0961

ANTHONY TAHLIER
USA
0962

HEATHER SPERLING
USA
0963

GALDONES PHOTOGRAPHY
USA

0964

ERIC KLEINBERG
USA

0965

GALDONES PHOTOGRAPHY
USA

0966

JACQUI WEDEWER
USA

0967

TY LETTAU
USA

0968

GALDONES PHOTOGRAPHY
USA

0969

GALDONES PHOTOGRAPHY
USA
0970

GALDONES PHOTOGRAPHY
USA
0971

GALDONES PHOTOGRAPHY
USA
0972

GALDONES PHOTOGRAPHY
USA
0973

0974

0975

0976

0977

ERIC KLEINBERG
USA

0978

GALDONES PHOTOGRAPHY
USA
0979

ERIC KLEINBERG
USA
0980

HEATHER SPERLING
USA
0981

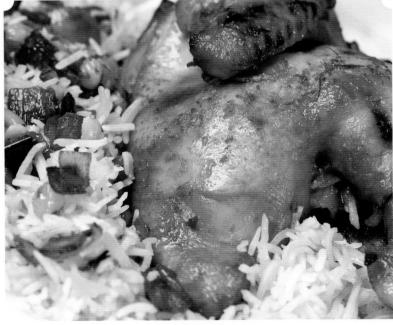

PARAGON MARKETING COMMUNICATIONS
KUWAIT
0982

PARAGON MARKETING COMMUNICATIONS
KUWAIT

0983

GALDONES PHOTOGRAPHY
USA

0984

GALDONES PHOTOGRAPHY
USA

0985

GALDONES PHOTOGRAPHY
USA

0986

NADINE SHAW
AUSTRALIA

0991

GRIP
USA
0992

GEORGIOS DETSIS
GREECE
0993

HEATHER SPERLING
USA
0994

GALDONES PHOTOGRAPHY
USA
0995

GRIP
USA

0996

GALDONES PHOTOGRAPHY
USA
0997

ANTHONY TAHLIER
USA
0998

ANDREW HICKEY
USA
0999

HEATHER SPERLING
USA
1000

INDEX

REFERENCE / QUICK-FIND / LOOK-UP / SOURCES / CREDITS

B

REGAN BARONI
2432 W. Haddon
Chicago, IL, 60622
612.396.2303
www.reganbaroni.com
reganbaroni@gmail.com

0061, 0209, 0470, 0913

EZEQUIEL BECERRA
Negrafix
Curridabat
San José
506.8813.6847
almakzumi@gmail.com

0014, 0332

ARI BENDERSKY
ari@ariwrites.com

0609, 0676, 0677, 0720, 0729, 0855, 0856, 0857, 0863, 0865

DAVE BRADLEY
Dave Bradley Photography
840 Summer St
Boston, MA, 02127
617.268.6644
www.davebradleyphoto.com
dave@davebradleyphoto.com

0001, 0308, 0893

TUAN H. BUI
1100 W. Cermak #B413
Oak Park, IL 60608
217.721.4455
http://tuanhbui.com
tuan@tuanhbui.com

0022, 0027, 0028, 0033, 0035, 0038, 0039, 0155, 0222, 0224,
0242, 0274, 0275, 0347, 0375, 0377, 0464, 0524, 0528–0534,
0579, 0584, 0595, 0597, 0599, 0657, 0659, 0660, 0666, 0687,
0734, 0758–0760, 0767, 0875, 0880, 0881, 0894

C

HEATHER CROSBY
YumUniverse.com
P.O. Box 3344
Shepherdstown, WV
773.220.2980
www.yumuniverse.com
yumuniverse@gmail.com

0203, 0278

D

ANDRES DANGOND
2615 W Berwyn St.
Lake Forest, CA, 92630
773.980.0106
www.andresdangond.com
andres@andresdangond.com

0145, 0185, 0488, 0521, 0906, 0909

MICHELLE DEITER
223 Thatcher Ave
River Forest, IL, 60305
708.969.0708
michelle@mbj3.com
michelledeiter@gmail.com

0068, 0073, 0129, 0205, 0253, 0306, 0381, 0419, 0437, 0513,
0541, 0802, 0803

RACHEL DE MARTE
2 S Leavitt, #206
Chicago, IL, 60612
773.963.5144
www.racheldemarte.com
rachel@racheldemarte.com

0132, 0481, 0678, 0688, 0814, 0884, 0912, 0956, 0958

GEORGIOS DETSIS
50 Chris Smirnis St.
Athens 15342
30.693740036
www.flickr/photos/giomio
georgios@detsis.net

0070, 0091, 0094, 0148, 0156, 0159, 0163, 0168, 0186, 0188,
1093, 0245–0247, 0329, 0351, 0450, 0501, 0503, 0507, 0508,
0661–0663, 0668, 0681, 0764, 0774, 0779, 0993

DAVID ROBERT ELLIOTT
John Coyle Steinbrunner Creatives, LLC
3828 N. Wilton
Chicago, IL, 60613
773.529.6880
www.jcsteinbrunner.com
jc@jcsteinbrunner.com

0689–0692

SCOTT ERB AND DONNA DUFAULT
Erb Photography
380 Bridle Path
Worcester, MA, 01604
508.421.3912
www.erbphoto.com
scott@erbphoto.com

0006, 0054, 0089, 0090, 0218, 0414, 0467, 0471, 0542, 0623, 0757, 0770, 0862, 0868, 0873, 0897

F

BRANDON FREITAS DESIGN
124 Potomska St.
New Bedford, MA, 02740
508.728.7994
www.BrandonFreitas.com
brandonfreitasdesign@gmail.com

0353, 0355, 0356, 0364, 0439, 0441, 0442, 0620, 0705

LUKASZ FUKS
Poludniowa 15/4
Pabianice
48.603.531.626
www.lukaszfuks.pl
lukasz.fuks@gmail.com

0497, 0627, 0740–0742, 0858

G

GALDONES PHOTOGRAPHY
720 N Larrabee St, #1410
Chicago, IL, 60654
617.922.4363
www.galdones.com
huge@galdones.com

0011, 0096, 0133, 0134, 0162, 0172, 0252, 0257, 0272, 0276, 0282, 0283, 0286, 0287, 0289, 0318, 0319, 0358, 0371, 0397, 0403, 0405, 0444, 0445, 0452–0459, 0463, 0484, 0487, 0490–0494, 0509, 0518, 0543–0545, 0547–0550, 0560, 0561, 0563, 0565–0567, 0569–0576, 0598, 0612, 0613, 0644, 0645, 0647–0651, 0656, 0670, 0684, 0701, 0702, 0754–0756, 0763, 0771, 0772, 0775, 0778, 0780, 0804, 0895, 0896, 0916–0918, 0920–0922, 0927, 0930, 0933, 0934, 0945–0949, 0964, 0966, 0969–0975, 0977, 0979, 0984–0990, 0995, 0997

GRIP
1128 N. Ashland Ave.
Chicago, IL 60622
312.906.8020
www.gripdesign.com
info@gripdesign.com

0016, 0053, 0207, 0228, 0305, 0310–0311, 0314, 0342–0346, 0348, 0350, 0443, 0446–0449, 0472–0449, 0551, 0605, 0671, 0685, 0686, 0704, 0727, 0728, 0752, 0762, 0792, 0931, 0942, 0992, 0996

H

ANDREW HICKEY
4512 N. Malden St.
Chicago, IL, 60640
773.944.5121
drewinchicago@gmail.com

0116, 0120, 0123, 0124, 0153, 0248, 0249, 0250, 0334, 0349, 0354, 0421, 0466, 0554, 0709, 0711, 0713, 0800, 0805, 0807, 0808, 0809, 0811, 0824, 0866, 0955, 0957, 0999

AZITA HOUSHIAR
917.379.8857
www.figandquince.com
fig@figandquince.com

0030, 0057, 0059, 0137, 0144, 0157, 0582, 0588, 0679, 0783, 0788

N

CARA AND SCOTT NAVA
Carasco Photography
1750 W 35th St.
Chicago, IL, 60609
773.383.4112
www.carascophoto.com
caranava@photocarasco.com

0015, 0192, 0264, 0330, 0331, 0352, 0374, 0420, 0511, 0522, 0535, 0669, 0672, 0784, 0790, 0810, 0877, 0879, 0887, 0919, 0923, 0976

P

PARAGON MARKETING COMMUNICATIONS
Al Hamad Tower A, 3rd Floor, Jibla, Behind Sheraton
PO Box 6097, Salmiya, 22071
965.2297440 / 22974388
www.paragonmc.com
info@paragonmc.com

0026, 0031, 0043, 0048, 0092, 0097, 0103, 0104, 0110, 0111, 0113–0115, 0122, 0125–0128, 0130 0138, 0149–0151, 0169, 0173, 0210, 0213–0215, 0217, 0235–0237, 0260–0263, 0285, 0288, 0290–0304, 0312, 0317, 0320–0328, 0361, 0363, 0365, 0367, 0369, 0384, 0386-0391, 0395, 0398–0402, 0404, 0407, 0412, 0418, 0426, 0431, 0435, 0438, 0440, 0482, 0483, 0500, 0525–0527, 0539, 0555–0559, 0682, 0719, 0721–0726, 0731, 0733, 0736, 0739, 0789, 0794, 0801, 0812, 0813, 0818–0819, 0822, 0823, 0825–836, 0838, 0839, 0869, 0870, 0885, 0886, 0888, 0889, 0891, 0939, 0941, 0951, 0959, 0982, 0983

JUSTIN B. PARIS
Justin B. Paris Photography
905 Stonehurst Dr
Roselle, IL, 60172
630.270.9829
www.justinbparis.com
justin@justinbparis.com

0004, 0087, 0243, 0251, 0256, 0259, 0269, 0307, 0406, 0577, 0578, 0607, 0753

ALLAN PENN
Allan Penn Photography
33 Commercial St., Ste 3
Gloucester, MA 01930
978.283.7321
www.allanpenn.com
penn@allanpenn.com

0743–0747, 0871, 0900

LAUREN PODOLSKY
4907 Whitlock Ln
Mechanicsburg, PA, 17055
717.525.1320
www.saywhatyouneedtosayblog.com
Lpodolsky410@gmail.com

0198, 0199, 0212, 0232

BRIAN POREA
Brian Porea Photography
290 San Jose Avenue
San Francisco, CA, 94110
415.279.5478
bporea@gmail.com

0161, 0164, 0422, 0538, 0683, 0777, 0787, 0791

R

ELISABETTA REDAELLI
Photography by Elisabetta Redaelli
Via Alciato 21
Alzate Brianza (CO), Italy, 22040
3.9340226096e+011
www.flickr.com/photos/lillyred
elisabetta.redaelli1@gmail.com

0012, 0032, 0044, 0046, 0088, 0180, 0415, 0592, 0667, 0765, 0768, 0837

SARA REMINGTON
1660 N. La Salle, #809
Chicago, IL, 60614
312.643.5614
constancepik@gmail.com

0158, 0309, 0360

CARLOS RIBEIRO
Sevenfiles
Rua Senhora da Guia, n° 110
4785-122 Trofa
3.519162661e+011
www.sevenfiles.com
carlosribeiro@sevenfiles.com

0072, 0231, 0610

KATE RIESENBERG
178 Atlantic Ave, #2
Brooklyn, NY, 11201
973.609.2034
www.mycitybites.wordpress.com
kate.riese@gmail.com

0005, 0083, 0085, 0095, 0117, 0136, 0139–0141, 0146, 0166,
0194–0196, 0208, 0244, 0254, 0335, 0336, 0366, 0479, 0499,
0519, 0587, 0665, 0697, 0700, 0708, 0730, 0751, 0786, 0795–
0799, 0860, 0867, 0876

BERNADINE ROLNICKI
195 N Harbor Drive 3401
Chicago, IL, 60601
312.213.8508
bernadine1018@aol.com

0062, 0121, 0183, 0184, 0191, 0496, 0664, 0766

ROOT STUDIO
The Terrace, Grantham St
Lincoln, Lincolnshire, LN2 1BD
01522 . 528246
www.rootstudio.co.uk
tom@rootstudio.co.uk

0716–0718

S

RONNIE SAINI
Ronnie Saini Design
215 Arboretum Way
Burlington, MA
781.640.9375
www.ronniesainiphotography.com
ronnie@ronniesainidesign.com

0176, 0216, 0859

LAURA SANT
891 Bergen St., Apt 3R
Brooklyn, NY, 11238
804.350.6409
www.mizsant.net
mizsant@gmail.com

0230, 0516

MARTA SASINOWSKA
YumUniverse.com
P.O. Box 3344
Shepherdstown, WV
773.220.2980
www.yumuniverse.com
yumuniverse@gmail.com

0202, 0642, 0652–0654

GLENN SCOTT
GSP, INC.
228 Cabot St.
Beverly, MA, 01915
978.927.5522
www.glennscottphotography.com
gsphotography@comcast.net

0025, 0219, 0429, 0430, 0433, 0776, 0872, 0937, 0950

RENATO SEALY
Leinster Rd, Waterford
St. Michael
246.249.0202
www.renatosealy.com
ren23egade@gmail.com

0630

NADINE SHAW
Nadine Shaw Photography
P.O. Box 838
Spring Hill, QLD, 4004
0413 . 748132
www.feastphotography.com.au
dine@feastphotography.com.au

0009, 0023, 0052, 0055, 0084, 0206, 0229, 0277, 0424, 0514,
0553, 0580, 0589, 0594, 0603, 0628, 0675, 0714, 0715, 0806, 0991

SHERI SILVER
Donuts, Dresses and Dirt
3 Cedarlawn Road
Irvington, NY, 10533
914.591.2679
www.sherisilver.com
sheri@sherisilver.com

0041, 0101, 0227, 265, 0271, 0280, 0316, 0393, 0425, 0636,
0639, 0673, 0674, 0710, 0845, 0849, 0853, 0907

KARI SKAFLEN
2101 W. Rice St., #105
Chicago, IL, 60622
312.451.3588
kari.skaflen@gmail.com

0187, 0333, 0379, 0480, 0498, 0505, 0864

ALYSA SLAY
205 Barberry Rd
Highland Park, IL, 60035
312.215.1114
aslay@sbcglobal.net

0270, 0634

HEATHER SPERLING
2623 N. Emmett St., #1
Chicago, IL, 60647
301.706.2934
www.heathersperling.com
heathersperling@gmail.com

0002, 0024, 0037, 0050, 0056, 0063, 0064, 0067, 0071, 0086,
0098–0100, 0102, 0105, 0107, 0108, 0112, 0131, 0147, 0152,
0177–0179, 0190, 0201, 0220, 0221, 0223, 0225, 0226, 0233,
0338-00341, 0362, 0376, 0380, 0392, 0394, 0408–0410, 0428,
0465, 0489, 0495, 0502, 0515, 0536, 0546, 0562, 0600–0602,
0626, 0732, 0749, 0750, 0843, 0846–0848, 0861, 0883, 0892,
0898, 0899, 0901–0905, 0908, 0925, 0940, 0953, 0954, 0963,
0981, 0994, 1000

T

ANTHONY TAHLIER
Anthony Tahlier Photography, Inc
2021 West Fulton
Chicago, IL, 60612
312.927.8669
www.anthonytahlier.com
info@anthonytahlier.com

0337, 0370, 0378, 0383, 0385, 0411, 0413, 0436, 0486, 0564,
0593, 0621, 0622, 0624, 0632, 0633, 0635, 0698, 0735, 0841,
0844, 0924, 0962, 0998

THAIN LIN TAY
50 Bt Batok East Avenue 5 #23-08
Singapore
6597828618
www.flickr.com/photos/tiny_tots/
thainlin@gmail.com

0142, 0143, 0154, 0189, 0878

V

HEATHER VAN GAALE
The Confection Oven
12405 Conquistador Way
San Diego, CA 92128
858.945.4218
www.theconfectionoven.com
info@theconfectionoven.com

0003, 0042, 0047, 0631, 0637, 0638, 0748, 0840, 0851, 0852

NANDY VILLONGCO
50pov.com
27 Avignon Avenue
Foothill Ranch, CA, 92610
949.292.7170
www.50pov.com
nandyv@notebookdrives.com

0658, 0761

W

JACQUI WEDEWER
Check, Please!
848 W. Eastman, #205
Chicago, IL, 60642
312.804.5561
jacqui@checkplease.tv

0106, 0504, 0952, 0960, 0967

Z

NICOLE ZARATE
121 W. 17th St.
Lombard, IL, 60143
415.828.5861
www.nicolezaratephoto.com
nicole@nicolezaratephoto.com

0040, 0066, 0082, 0255, 0268, 0423, 0512, 0643

ABOUT

THE AUTHOR

Ari Bendersky, a longtime food and wine writer, is currently the director of content and editor in chief for AbesMarket.com, a mindful living destination for natural and organic products, news, and information. Prior to joining Abe's, Ari was the founding editor of Eater Chicago and built it into the No. 1 destination for restaurant news in Chicago. During the course of his lengthy career, Ari has also covered music, lifestyle, and travel, writing for the *New York Times*, Associated Press, RollingStone.com, *Chicago* magazine, Saveur.com, and more.